Lunka's Trumpet

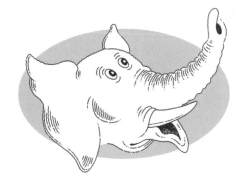

By John Parker

Illustrated by Gillian Chapman

DOMINIE PRESS

Pearson Learning Group

Publisher: Raymond Yuen
Project Editor: John S. F. Graham
Editor: Bob Rowland
Designer: Greg DiGenti
Illustrator: Gillian Chapman

Published by:

ﻌ Dominie Press, Inc.

1949 Kellogg Avenue
Carlsbad, California 92008 USA

www.dominie.com

1-800-232-4570

Paperback ISBN 0-7685-1628-5
Printed in Singapore by PH Productions Pte Ltd
   4 5 6 PH 05

Table of Contents

Chapter One
Six O'clock in the Morning

Lunka was a small elephant. And like all elephants, she had a long and leathery trunk.

Every morning at exactly six o'clock, she pointed her long, leathery trunk at the sun.

Then she took a deep breath until she was almost twice her normal size. Then she blew through her trunk as hard as she could.

TOOT-TOOT-TOOT-TOO!!

It sounded like the biggest trumpet in the world.

The animals in the jungle liked Lunka's trumpet because it woke them up.

The parrots squawked.

The monkeys chattered.

The lions stretched.

The hippopotamuses splashed.

The frogs jumped.

"That's Lunka's trumpet," they said to each other. "Time to start another day!"

However, Tatso, the grumpy tiger, didn't like Lunka's trumpet. Tatso didn't want to be awakened at six o'clock in the morning. He wanted to sleep in.

So he called a big meeting and complained to all the animals.

"But we like it," they said. "It keeps us on our toes."

"You mean paws," sniffed Tatso.

"Talking about paws," said a monkey, "why don't you sleep with your paws over your ears? Then you wouldn't hear Lunka's trumpet."

"That's not funny," snapped Tatso.

"Well," said the animals. "It's not funny stopping Lunka's trumpet, either."

Chapter Two
Tiger Fibs

Tatso didn't listen. He ran up to Lunka beside the river, just as she was about to squirt herself with water from her trunk.

"The animals say you have to stop your morning trumpet," he said.

Lunka was so surprised, she

accidentally squirted the water all over Tatso, instead.

"Sorry," said Lunka, as Tatso tried to shake off all the water. "I got such a surprise."

"Well," said Tatso angrily, "that's the way it is now—no more trumpets."

"I thought the animals liked my trumpet," Lunka said. She shook her head sadly. "When do I have to stop?"

"Now!" shouted Tatso. "That's what the animals said."

"But I'm an elephant," said Lunka. "Elephants are supposed to make trumpet calls."

"Too bad," sneered Tatso. He looked at the frogs sitting in the sun on the water lilies. "Be a frog," he said.

Lunka opened her eyes wide. "Really?"

"Yes," said Tatso. "That's what all the animals said. Be a frog!"

He giggled as he trotted away. "That's the end of her silly trumpet," he said. "Now I can sleep late! Ha, ha!"

Chapter Three
Horrible Croaks!

However, the next morning a horrible noise woke up Tatso.

CRRRRROOOOOOOAK!

It sounded like a thousand frogs with bad colds, all trying to croak at the same time. Tatso said to himself, "It can't be

13

Lunka, can it?"

He hurried to the river—and it *was* Lunka. Covered with green water lily leaves, she was crouching beside the frogs on the riverbank.

"Hello, Tatso," she said. "I'm a frog. I'm sitting like a frog, and I'm green like a frog."

She stood up and bent her legs. "Now I'm going to hop like a frog."

"No!" screamed Tatso, but he was too late. Lunka hopped as high as she could and landed on the ground beside the tiger.

BOOOOOOOOOOOOM!

The ground shook like a trampoline and bounced Tatso into the top of a tall tree.

"Sorry," said Lunka.

"Help!" yelled Tatso. "Use your trunk

to pull the tree toward the ground!"

"Sorry, I don't have a trunk," said Lunka. "I'm a frog."

So Tatso had to climb all the way down by himself.

Chapter Four
Water Everywhere

"**H**ave you seen me jump just like a frog onto a water lily?" Lunka asked, once Tatso reached the ground.

"No!" shouted Tatso. "And I don't want to!"

He was too late. Lunka jumped.

She crashed through the water lily and into the river. Most of the river splashed over Tatso. It made him grumpier than ever.

"Silly elephant!" he said.

"I'm not an elephant," said Lunka. "I'm a frog."

Then she frowned. "I'm not a very good frog, though. I need more practice at jumping on water lily leaves."

"No, *no*! *Noooooooooooooo!*" screamed Tatso—but, again, he was too late.

Lunka thumped down the hill and threw herself high into the air. Tatso ran away as fast as he could. But this time the splash was so big that it sent one hippopotamus and nine frogs over Tatso, as well as lots of water.

Tatso wriggled out from under the hippopotamus and shook off the frogs.

He scowled. His tail twitched. "I'm grumpy!" he shouted.

"I thought you were Tatso," said Lunka.

"Not funny!" said Tatso, looking grumpier than ever.

Chapter Five
Lunka Trumpets Again

"**I** can't stay to talk," said Lunka.
"Being a frog is harder than I thought.
I've got to practice croaking for an hour."

It was too much for Tatso. Still
dripping with water, the tiger walked
slowly over to Lunka.

He hung his head. "I pretended that the animals didn't like your morning trumpet. They really do like your trumpet. And they don't want you to be a frog. That was my idea."

Tatso walked off slowly, while Lunka danced with delight. "*Wheeeeeeee!*" she said. "Tomorrow morning I'm going to give the biggest trumpet the jungle has ever heard!"

Tatso hung his head. He knew he would not be getting much sleep.

Sure enough, the next morning at six o'clock, Lunka pointed her long, leathery trunk at the sun and blew as hard as she could.

TOOT-TOOT-TOOT-TOO!!

"Hurray," said all the animals. "Lunka's back again!"

For once, though, Tatso slept through

Lunka's trumpet.

The monkeys had given him a sleep-in present—two bananas, one in each ear.